Vegan Smoothies Cookbook

Detox Your Body With These Delicious Smoothies, Juicing Recipes & Tips For a Longer, Healthier Life (2022 Guide for Beginners)

Echo Cooke

CONTENTS

INTRODUCTION

"YOU'RE VEGAN? WHAT DO YOU EVEN EAT?"

You've probably heard this question 101 times since making the ethical and sustainable decision to go vegan. "Umm... stuff that doesn't come from animals?" is most likely your response.

People are frequently taken aback by this, but the truth is that a lot of food is already vegan—and with a little imagination and the correct ingredients, you can vegan-ify practically anything else.

People frequently believe that being vegan is restrictive or a diet, however, this is not the case. Most vegans enjoy eating; they simply prioritize their ethics and principles when deciding what to eat.

If you're new to vegan cooking, you might have some questions, so read the introduction before diving into the delicious and simple recipes in this book for tips, tricks, and useful information.

"Where do you get your protein?"

This is yet another vexing subject that vegans are frequently asked. People act as though meat and dairy are the only protein sources on the planet!

In reality, most people in wealthy countries consume far too much protein. If you're new to the vegan diet, you should spend some time calculating protein and planning your meals to ensure you're receiving enough, but protein insufficiency is uncommon.

Amino acids are chemical substances that are involved in a wide range of bodily activities. Proteins are formed when amino acids join together in long chains. While our bodies can synthesize numerous amino acids on their own, there are nine forms that the human body cannot produce. This means that we must rely on our meals to meet these requirements.

Vegans should bear in mind that not all protein sources include all of the amino acids that they require. In truth, the majority do not. But don't worry: as long as you have all of these amino acids in one day, you should be good.

That implies you can't rely on just one or two kinds of protein per day. When eating vegan, a good rule of thumb is to include two types of protein in each meal. This may appear to be a hassle, but you'd be amazed at how many foods contain protein. You won't even think about getting adequate protein once you've gotten used to eating a vegan diet and creative cooking.

Find out how many grams of protein you should consume per day by consulting a dietitian or searching online. To make things easier, each recipe in this cookbook specifies the number of grams of protein in a serving.

If you're tired of answering the protein question, take a look at five popular vegan proteins, how to use them, and their nutritional benefits.

Beans, black

Did you know that the darker the color of a bean, the higher the number of antioxidants it contains? Black beans are unquestionably a vegan staple. With 15 grams of protein and 15 grams of fiber per cooked cup, black beans are a terrific way to make a meal more substantial. This cookbook contains numerous dishes that incorporate this hearty bean, ranging from Mexican meals to brownies (yes, brownies).

Walnuts

Vegans can also get protein from nuts and seeds. This nut, which is high in healthy fats and protein, is a terrific snack or complement to a meal to help you feel full. Crush walnuts and add them to sweets, pasta, or even pizza!

Quinoa

Quinoa may be the vegan protein king. This seed (yes, quinoa is actually a seed, but it's served as a grain) was once consumed by Incan warriors and provided a full amino acid group. That implies you won't have to worry about combining proteins if you consume quinoa. Quinoa is delicious in salads, as a veggie burger, or with curry. Quinoa spaghetti is even available at your local health food store.

Chickpeas

This adaptable bean can be used for more than just hummus (although hummus is a delicious vegan staple you should master). Chickpeas provide 14.5 grams of protein per cooked cup, as well as 11 grams of fiber, manganese, and folate, an important nutrient for women. Chickpeas are delicious in curries, salads, stews, and a variety of other dishes.

Oats

There's no vegan breakfast quite like cinnamon and brown sugar oatmeal, and that's not even the best part about oats. Oats have been shown to help lower cholesterol, so if you turned vegan for your heart health (a wise decision), you should incorporate oats into your diet whenever possible. Gluten-free? Not to worry! Gluten-free oats and oat flour are widely available.

Tofu

Tofu, made from soybeans, is a vegan favorite, yet most non-vegans dislike it. Why has tofu earned such a nasty rap? Who knows, but maybe your carnivorous pals may become tofu fans after trying the dishes in this book. No vegan diet is complete without tofu, which has only 178 calories per serving but 12 grams of protein. Bread, fry, bake, or combine it; the options are unlimited, so get creative with this protein-packed delight.

Buy GMO-free tofu since the health effects of eating genetically modified soybeans are unknown.

Lentils

Lentils are a bean that appears in cuisines all across the world, from French to Indian, and frequently in this cookbook. Lentils, which contain 18 grams of protein per cooked cup, are an excellent complement to stews, vegetarian burgers, salads, and meat substitutes.

"Can you eat this?"

Yes, is a quick response to this question. As a vegan, you are theoretically allowed to eat anything; you simply choose not to. Whether you became a vegan for health, weight reduction, the environment, your love of animals, or all of the above, don't allow your lifestyle choice to limit you. Eating vegan may, with some practice and imagination, open new doors to culinary delights rather than close them.

"Is this really vegan?"

When dining at a vegan restaurant, you may find yourself asking this question. How do they make cuisine that is creamy, buttery, or cheesy without the use of dairy? Vegan hacks are the answer. Every vegan should be familiar with a few pantry basics. These essentials aid in recreating flavors that aren't typically associated with a plant-based diet.

Once you've mastered these components, your next dinner party will be greeted with a chorus of "Is this actually vegan?"

Cashews

Cashews are a must-have in any vegan pantry. Soak them for a few hours in the water, then drain and combine with herbs and spices to make creamy dipping sauces, or with sugar and chocolate powder to make vegan ice cream. The high-protein options are nearly limitless. Does anyone for cashew "milk" shake?

Yeast Nutritional

Because nutritional yeast has a cheesy flavor, it is the first choice of most vegans when it comes to cheese substitutes. With only 40 calories and 3 grams of protein per tablespoon, it's low in calories but high in protein. Most vegans simply cannot live without nutritional yeast, and shops are well aware of this; as a result, it is frequently fortified with vitamins that vegans commonly lack, such as vitamin B12. Why bother taking a multivitamin when you can have creamy, delicious vegan queso every day?

Tahini

Tahini, like cashews and nutritional yeast, is an easy method to boost protein in a meal. It's also high in good fats. Tahini adds richness as well as a nutty taste to recipes, making it an excellent addition to curries and stir-fries. Tahini is also an excellent base for salad dressings and glazes. If you have a nut allergy, you can substitute tahini for nuts in a variety of dishes.

Avocado

Another technique to add creaminess to recipes is to use avocado. Avocado is as healthy as it is delicious, with 13 grams of fiber and 4 grams of protein per serving. Avocados can be used to produce a delicious chocolate mousse or a decadent pasta sauce. To make a smoothie even creamier, add an avocado.

Seeds of Flax

Flax seeds are a simple method to boost protein in any dish. Flax seeds are particularly abundant in omega fatty acids, which are essential for healthy skin. Simply toss some ground flax seeds into a smoothie for an instant energy boost. Doctors also recommend incorporating omega fatty acids into your diet during the winter, along with vitamin D, to combat the winter blues.

As if that weren't enough, these tiny seeds are also an excellent egg substitute. A tablespoon of ground flax seeds combined with a tablespoon of water yields a quick egg substitute that can be used in practically any recipe.

Because your body cannot absorb entire flax seeds, make sure you get ground flax seeds.

Cauliflower

Cauliflower is a low-carbohydrate substitute for rice, potatoes, and even wheat, making it one of the most adaptable vegetables on the planet. Cauliflower is inexpensive in calories but abundant in vitamin C, making it a nutritional winner. Cauliflower becomes extremely creamy when boiled and combined, making it an ideal nutrient-dense cream substitute.

Replace heavy cream in soups and curries, or use it to make "cheese."

"Is being vegan expensive?"

Some specialty goods may be more expensive, but following a vegan diet does not have to be a costly endeavor. Which is normally more expensive at the grocery store, meat or vegetables?

The greatest method to save money on a vegan diet is to shop at local farmers' markets and buy seasonal products. Buying from local farmers not only benefits your community but is also better for the environment because the product does not have to travel large distances.

Check out this seasonal vegetable guide.

Pomegranate, butternut squash, apples, pears, figs, sweet potatoes, arugula, beets, peppers, broccoli, celery, eggplant, cranberries, potatoes, lettuce, mushrooms, limes, pumpkins, green beans, and zucchini

Winter vegetables include beets, cabbage, oranges, Brussels sprouts, onions, clementines, kale, cauliflower, leeks, grapefruit, lemons, mandarin oranges, shallots, radishes, turnips, winter squash, and tangerines.

Asparagus, strawberries, cherries, rhubarb, kumquats, fava beans, apricots, chard, kiwis, new potatoes, peas, spinach, and spring onions

Avocados, peaches, cantaloupes, blackberries, mangos, bell peppers, lemongrass, chard, blueberries, okra, chickpeas, melons, collard greens, grapes, cucumbers, figs, plums, raspberries, spinach, watermelons, summer squash, nectarines

Organic produce is frequently more expensive than conventional produce, but it is better for the environment and your body because it is free of hazardous pesticides and other chemicals. That being said, eating entirely organic produce isn't always necessary.

Experts have created lists known as the Clean 15 and the Dirty Dozen. The Clean 15 are the 15 fruits and vegetables with the lowest pesticide levels and are thus safe to eat even if they are not organic. The Dirty Dozen are the 12 fruits and vegetables that contain the most chemicals. You should avoid eating these unless they are organic.

Corn, pineapple, cauliflower, honeydew, avocado, kiwi, onions, eggplant, cabbage, sweet peas, asparagus, papaya, mangos, cantaloupe, and grapefruit are among the Clean 15.

The infamous "Dirty Dozen"
Spinach, pears, strawberries, bell peppers, celery, nectarines, potatoes, cherries, apples, grapes, peaches, and tomatoes are all good choices.

"Is being vegan a lot of work?"
Being a vegan takes as much effort as you want it to. Many vegans regard their diet as a hobby as well as a way of life. Vegan cooking is enjoyable and creative, so if you see your vegan friends cooking for hours every day, it's generally because they enjoy preparing and eating beautiful, healthy meals, not because they have to.

Being a vegan can be a simple and low-maintenance lifestyle. Many of the dishes in this book don't even call for cooking and may be prepared in 10 minutes or less.

Being a vegan is a lot of fun now since there are so many delicious and nutritional options. As an added benefit, vegan food is typically lower in calories, allowing you to enjoy seemingly rich meals without jeopardizing your health or waistline.

Why would you eat meat or dairy when vegan food can be this healthy and delicious?

Smoothie Tips

Smoothies are a terrific way to pack a nutritional punch into your day with minimal effort in the kitchen. If you want to incorporate smoothies into your routine or detox regimen, read on.

Replace Coffee

It's no secret that drinking a lot of caffeine in the morning can make you jittery all day. It also makes you crash in the afternoon, creating an endless cycle of caffeine addiction. Coffee may instantly perk you up, but drinking too much has an acidic effect on the body and wreaks havoc on your digestive system.

The answer? Replace your morning coffee with a healthy, nutrientdense smoothie. A green smoothie with protein in the morning is guaranteed to jump-start your digestive system and metabolism and give you sustained energy for hours.

Think Outside the Box

Think smoothies are just for fruit? Think again! Herbs, tea, spices, nut butters, seeds, veggies and greens all make great additions to smoothies. Next time you have veggies in the fridge about to go bad, just throw them into your morning smoothie!

Smoothies are more than just breakfast, though. A well-thought-out smoothie with protein can make for an easy meal any time you don't have time to cook. They're also a great option as an afternoon snack for the kids.

On a diet, but still love dessert? Vegan smoothies are your answer. This cookbook features a whole section of dessert smoothies and another on smoothie bowls. With all of these options, there's no need to deny your sweet tooth!

Meal Prep

Meal prepping can change your life. If you think you don't have time to make healthy meals, meal prepping is the answer. At the beginning of the week, plan the smoothies you want to make. Put all of the ingredients, already cut and measured, into a Ziploc bag or Mason jar (more sustainable). That way, whenever you want a healthy meal or snack, you just dump the entire contents into the blender and serve.

Embrace Your Freezer

Freezing fruits and veggies that are nearing their expiration date is a great way to save money and avoid waste, and they also make great additions to smoothies. Use a cup of frozen berries in place of ice in a recipe for some extra fiber and antioxidants.

Frozen bananas are especially useful because they not only deliver potassium and fiber but can also serve as a great base for a thick and creamy smoothie bowl. Frozen bananas can totally amp up your smoothie game, and the overripe ones are just perfect for this. Next time you're at the farmers' market, ask if you can buy some of the overripe bananas at a discount. Don't be afraid of brown spots! Adding banana to a smoothie often means that you don't need to add sweetener.

Taste First

None of the recipes in this cookbook call for refined sugar or artificial flavors, but even natural sweeteners can be high in sugar and calories. Before you sweeten your smoothie, it's a good idea to taste it first—you may find it's perfect just the way it is.

About Sweeteners

Some individuals enjoy very sweet smoothies, while others prefer something milder, so alter the sweetness level of all of the smoothies in this cookbook to your liking. If you want sweet smoothies, check out these natural vegan sweeteners. There's no need to include highly addicting refined sugar in any of these recipes.

Maple Syrup

All-natural maple syrup is one of Mother Nature's best gifts. Its pleasing sweetness is complemented by a subtle earth flavor. Maple syrup is great in any recipe, but goes especially well with dessert smoothies. Maple syrup pairs nicely with warm spices like cinnamon, ginger, and chai tea. It also goes great with fall flavors like butternut squash or pumpkin. Unlike sugar, maple syrup is high in antioxidants and helps to reduce inflammation. While those with irritable bowel syndrome usually have to avoid honey, 100% vegan maple syrup is safe for them to eat. When shopping for maple syrup, be sure to read the ingredients list, because some "maple syrups" in the grocery store may be made in part or entirely of corn syrup and artificial flavors!

Dates

These Middle Eastern delights are one of the healthiest sweeteners and make a great addition to any smoothie. Add one or more depending on how sweet you'd like your smoothie, but be sure to pit your dates before you add them to the blender. Dates are also a natural energy booster, so eat them in the morning or before a workout!

Fruit Juice

All-natural fruit juice can add the sweetness you need to a smoothie while also providing the liquid that makes it easier to blend. Just make sure your fruit juice doesn't have any added sugar. Opt for juices like orange or apple if you're on a budget. If not, pomegranate or acai juice can add much-needed antioxidants and some unique flavor. Coconut water is another great option for something more tropical!

Bananas

Bananas make for a sweetener filled with fiber and much-needed minerals and vitamins. Bananas are loaded with magnesium, so add one after a workout or when you're on your period

Blackstrap Molasses

Molasses is an antioxidant-dense, low-glycemic sweetener.

Molasses is especially high in iron, a nutrient that vegans often lack, so menstruating or pregnant women should consider integrating this sweetener into their meals.

Simple Smoothies

GRANOLA SMOOTHIE

This granola smoothie is a great option for breakfast. Granola adds flavorful crunch along with cholesterol-lowering fiber, while butternut squash is loaded with vitamin A and nut butter adds heart-healthy fat and protein.

Yields: 2 – Prep. Time: 5 min. – Cooking Time: 0 min.

Ingredients
1 apple
1 pear
½ cup vegan milk, vanilla
¼ cup roasted butternut squash 1 tablespoon nut butter
¼ cup granola, cinnamon flavored
1 tablespoon maple syrup (if desired)
Ice

Preparation

1. Combine all ingredients except the granola and blend until smooth. Slowly add milk as needed.

2. When the smoothie is blended to your desired consistency, add granola and pulse for a few seconds. You just want to mix it in a little.

Nutrition facts per serving:
Calories 246, total fat 7 g, carbs 44 g,
Protein 7 g, sodium 48 mg

GINGER BERRY

This smoothie is so simple, but it's loaded with nutrients. Mixed berries bring to the table fiber, antioxidants, and vitamin C, while fresh ginger is a great anti-inflammatory. Ground flaxseed adds healthy fats that make your skin glow! This smoothie is perfect if you feel like you're getting sick. If your mixed berries aren't frozen, that's OK: just add some ice instead.

Yields: 2 – Prep. Time: 5 min. – Cooking Time: 0 min.

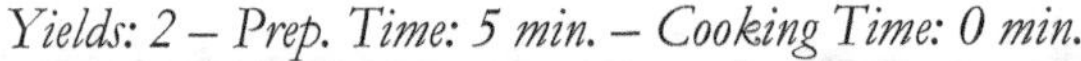

Ingredients

1 cup mixed berries, frozen
1 tablespoon fresh ginger, grated
½ cup apple juice
1 tablespoon flaxseeds

Preparation

1. Combine all ingredients and blend until smooth. Slowly add juice as needed.

Nutrition facts per serving:

Calories 92, total fat 2 g, carbs 19 g,
Protein 1 g, sodium 4 mg

PINK PRINCESS

The beautiful pink color of this smoothie is a great way to convince your picky princess to eat her daily fruit and veggie servings. Beets deliver a bright pink color plus sweetness, not to mention fiber, antioxidants, and vitamin C. This is also a great smoothie for pregnant women, because beets have much-needed folate. Topped with vegan whipped cream, this is a delightful treat.

Yields: 4 – Prep. Time: 5 min. – Cooking Time: 0 min.

Ingredients
1 red apple, Honeycrisp recommended
1 cup strawberries ½ cup raspberries
½ cup beets, cooked
1 banana
½ cup water (or as needed)
Vegan whipped cream
Ice

Preparation
1. Combine all ingredients and blend until smooth. Slowly add water and ice as needed.
2. Top with whipped cream and serve.

Nutrition facts per serving:
Calories 126, total fat 4 g, carbs 24 g,
Protein 2 g, sodium 123 mg

BANANA NUT

This smoothie tastes like banana bread, but with less carbs. It can even be made as a gluten-free alternative to banana bread. Nuts and flaxseed serve up protein and healthy fats that will keep you feeling satiated for hours. Bananas provide fiber and potassium for a heart-healthy treat.

Yields: 2 – Prep. Time: 5 min. – Cooking Time: 0 min.

Ingredients 2 bananas
¼ cup granola
1 cup vegan milk, vanilla
¼ cup chopped nuts of choice, unsalted (plus more for topping)
1 tablespoon flaxseed
Vegan whipped cream
Cinnamon (to taste)
Ice

Preparation

1. Combine all ingredients, except for the granola, and blend until smooth. Slowly add ice and milk as needed.

2. When the smoothie is blended to your desired consistency, add granola and pulse for a few seconds. You just want to mix it in a little.

3. Top with whipped cream, crushed nuts, and cinnamon

Nutrition facts per serving:
Calories 366, total fat 20 g, carbs 45 g,
Protein 9 g, sodium 31 mg

CHOCOLATE KICKSTART

Drinking multiple cups of coffee every day is bad for your mood and digestive system, but that doesn't mean you have to cut coffee out entirely. This smoothie is a great option whether you're trying to wean yourself off of coffee or you just love mocha flavors. Plus, raw cocoa powder is ridiculously high in antioxidants.

Yields: 2 – Prep. Time: 5 min. – Cooking Time: 0 min.

Ingredients
1 banana, frozen
½ cup vegan milk
½ cup coffee, cold
1 tablespoon flaxseed
1 tablespoon nut butter (optional)
2 tablespoons cocoa powder (or chocolate protein powder)
1 tablespoon maple syrup

Preparation

1. Combine all ingredients and blend until smooth. Slowly add milk as needed.

Nutrition facts per serving:

Calories 178, total fat 8 g, carbs 27 g,
Protein 5 g, sodium 27 mg

PEACH CARROT

This smoothie is a bright idea when you're looking for something to use all of those summer peaches for! Carrots are high in vitamin A, very important for your skin and eyesight, while sweet peaches are loaded with antioxidants and vitamin C, making this easy smoothie a nutritional powerhouse.

Yields: 2 – Prep. Time: 5 min. – Cooking Time: 0 min.

Ingredients
½ cup shredded carrots
2 peaches, pitted
1 mango
1 cup apple juice or water
Ice

Preparation
1. Combine all ingredients and blend until smooth. Slowly add liquid as needed.

Nutrition facts per serving:
Calories 189, total fat 1 g, carbs 46 g,
Protein 2 g, sodium 49 mg

BANANA OATMEAL

Between fiber-filled oatmeal and banana, this smoothie couldn't be healthier for your heart. This smoothie actually has 12 grams of fiber per serving, which is more than a third of the fiber you need in a day! Plus, vegan yogurt delivers much-needed probiotics, making this smoothie a great choice for gut health too.

Yields: 2 – Prep. Time: 5 min. – Cooking Time: 0 min.

Ingredients
1 banana
½ cup vegan yogurt (coconut or soy)
½ cup vegan milk, vanilla
¼ cup rolled oats
1 tablespoon flaxseed
1 date, pitted
Ice

Preparation
1. Combine all ingredients and blend until smooth. Slowly add ice as needed.

Nutrition facts per serving:
Calories 230, total fat 5 g, carbs 42 g,
Protein 7 g, sodium 40 mg

SNEAKY SMOOTHIE

This smoothie is perfect for tricking kids into eating their veggies. Sweet berries, high in antioxidants, cover up the taste of matchstick carrots, which deliver vitamin A and fiber.

Yields: 4 – Prep. Time: 5 min. – Cooking Time: 0 min.

Ingredients
1 cup strawberries
½ cup mixed berries
½ cup (or to taste) matchstick or shredded carrots
1 cup vegan milk, unsweetened
1 banana
Ice

Preparation
1. Combine all ingredients and blend until smooth. Slowly add ice as needed.

Nutrition facts per serving:
Calories 80, total fat 1 g, carbs 16 g,
Protein 3 g, sodium 45 mg

Superfood Smoothies

GLOWING SKIN

One of the best things you can do to get glowing skin is eating a high fiber diet, because fiber helps your body remove toxins that lead to acne. Papaya is one of the best individual foods for your skin because it is rich in antioxidants, vitamin A, and an enzyme called papain. Papain is a coveted enzyme often seen in face products, and it also improves your digestion. Pineapple is another great treat for your skin. It contains an anti-inflammatory enzyme called bromelain, so add pineapple to your diet if you're struggling with redness or cystic acne.

Yields: 4 — Prep. Time: 5 min. — Cooking Time: 0 min.

Ingredients 1 apple
½ cup pineapple
½ cup papaya
½ cup strawberry
¼ cup pomegranate seeds
¼ cup beets, peeled and cooked
1 cup orange juice
1 tablespoon flaxseed
Ice

Preparation

1. Combine all ingredients and blend until smooth. Slowly add ice and orange juice as needed.

Nutrition facts per serving:

Calories 109, total fat 1 g, carbs 24 g,
Protein 2 g, sodium 63 mg

RAINBOW SMOOTHIE

This smoothie is so beautiful that it's yet another way to coax kids into eating their fruits and veggies. Serve in a large Mason jar so you can see all of the colors. This smoothie may call for a lot of ingredients and a little more effort, but the results are picture perfect.

Plus, with chia seeds, turmeric, and spirulina, it's crazy healthy. Spirulina in particular is a superfood that helps to detoxify the body. It has even been shown to help patients suffering from HIV and cancer.

Yields: 4 – Prep. Time: 5 min. – Cooking Time: 0 min.

Ingredients
<u>Red</u>
¼ cup strawberries
¼ cup raspberries
1 apple
½ tablespoon maple syrup
½ tablespoon chia seeds
Coconut water (as needed)
Ice

<u>Orange</u>
1 peach
½ mango
¼ cup sweet potato
¼ teaspoon turmeric
Orange juice (as needed)
Ice

<u>Green</u>
½ cup spinach 1 kiwi
1 green apple
¼ cup pineapple
½ tablespoon maple syrup
Coconut water (as needed)
Ice

<u>Blue</u>
½ cup blueberries
½ cup blackberries
1 banana
1 teaspoon blue spirulina powder
½ tablespoon maple syrup
Coconut water (as needed)
Ice

Preparation

1. Combine ingredients for one color in the blender. Blend, slowly adding ice and liquid as needed. Pour into glasses, then clean the blender out between colors. Repeat until you've worked your way through all of the colors.

2. Makes 4 large servings.

Nutrition facts per serving:

Calories 210, total fat 1 g, carbs 50 g,
Protein 3 g, sodium 49 mg

CHAI TEA SMOOTHIE

Chai tea is filled with warming spices like cinnamon, ginger, and cardamom that are amazing for your digestive system. It has caffeine, too, so this smoothie can even be a great replacement for coffee in the morning!

Yields: 2 – Prep. Time: 5 min. – Cooking Time: 0 min.

Ingredients
¾ cup brewed chai tea
1 banana, frozen
½ cup coconut milk (or as needed)
2 tablespoons maple syrup
½ teaspoon vanilla extract

Preparation
1. Combine all ingredients and blend until smooth. Slowly add coconut milk as needed.

Nutrition facts per serving:
Calories 256, total fat 13 g, carbs 36 g,
Protein 3 g, sodium 31 mg

ORANGE POWER

This smoothie is jam-packed with vitamin A, which is great for preventing age-related eye conditions and also works wonders for your skin. Bright yellow turmeric may just be one of the most powerful spices; as a supercharged anti-inflammatory, turmeric is believed to help prevent cancer and Alzheimer's.

Yields: 2 – Prep. Time: 5 min. – Cooking Time: 0 min.

Ingredients 1 mango
1 peach
¼ cup shredded carrots
¼ cup sweet potato, peeled and cooked
1 cup orange juice
½ teaspoon turmeric
1 tablespoon maple syrup or 1 date, pitted
Ice

Preparation
1. Combine all ingredients and blend until smooth. Slowly add orange juice as needed.

Nutrition facts per serving:
Calories 264, total fat 1 g, carbs 64 g, Protein 4 g, sodium 117 mg

UNDER THE WEATHER SMOOTHIE

When you feel like you're getting sick, don't rush to the doctor to get costly antibiotics. Nature has plenty of antibiotics of its own! This smoothie is filled with all-natural antibiotics, like fresh ginger, *and* loaded with vitamin C, so don't skip this recipe come cold and flu season.

Yields: 2 – Prep. Time: 5 min. – Cooking Time: 0 min.

Ingredients
1 banana
1 tablespoon ginger, fresh
½ cup vegan yogurt
½ cup orange juice
1 cup mixed berries ½ lime, juiced
½ cup leafy greens
1 tablespoon chia seeds
1 date, pitted

Preparation
1. Combine all ingredients and blend until smooth. Slowly add orange juice as needed.

Nutrition facts per serving:
Calories 264, total fat 1 g, carbs 64 g,
Protein 4 g, sodium 117 mg

ALLERGY SEASON

Reducing allergy symptoms is all about eating natural antihistamines and anti-inflammatory foods like ginger, lemon, and green tea. Mint also serves as a natural antihistamine while thinning mucus in the body.

Yields: 2 – Prep. Time: 5 min. – Cooking Time: 0 min.

Ingredients
1 cup mixed berries
1 apple
1 cup green tea
1 lemon, juiced
¼ cup pomegranate seeds
¼ cup mint leaves
¼ cup kale
1 tablespoon ginger, fresh
1 tablespoon flaxseed
2 dates, pitted
Ice

Preparation
1. Combine all ingredients and blend until smooth. Slowly add green tea as needed.

Nutrition facts per serving:
Calories 165, total fat 2 g, carbs 39 g,
Protein 2 g, sodium 7 mg

DAILY DETOX

Each day we consume tons of toxins, from pollution in the air to chemicals in our beauty products to pesticides in our food. You may think that a detox is something you do every once in a while, but there are plenty of foods that can help you detox every day. Foods rich in fiber and antioxidants can help you avoid the rapid aging and immune system damage that comes from consuming too many toxins.

Yields: 2 – Prep. Time: 5 min. – Cooking Time: 0 min.

Ingredients

1 lemon, juiced
1 apple
1 cup pineapple
¼ cup beets, cooked and peeled
½ cup green tea
1 tablespoon ginger
1 tablespoon flaxseed
1 tablespoon maple syrup (if desired)
Ice

Preparation

1. Combine all ingredients and blend until smooth. Slowly add green tea as needed.

Nutrition facts per serving:

Calories 218, total fat 2 g, carbs 51 g,
Protein 3 g, sodium 127 mg

CHOCOLATE PROTEIN

The best way to start your morning is with protein. Protein keeps you feeling full longer and has been shown to help control appetite throughout the day. While chia seeds and nut butter are helping you stay full, raw cocoa powder serves as a super-powerful antioxidant— all the more reason to indulge in this creamy chocolate smoothie!

Yields: 2 – Prep. Time: 5 min. – Cooking Time: 0 min.

Ingredients
2 bananas
1 cup soy milk
2 tablespoons chia seeds
2 tablespoons nut butter
2–3 tablespoons raw cocoa powder or chocolate protein powder
¼ teaspoon cinnamon

Preparation
1. Combine all ingredients and blend until smooth. Slowly add milk as needed.

Nutrition facts per serving:
Calories 339, total fat 15 g, carbs 48 g,
Protein 10 g, sodium 80 mg

NUTS & DATES

Dates are not only sweet, but also a nutritional powerhouse bringing protein, iron, and B vitamins to the table. All these nutrients can be more difficult to get on a vegan diet, so be sure to add this smoothie to your day.

Yields: 2 – Prep. Time: 5 min. – Cooking Time: 0 min.

Ingredients
2 bananas
1 cup vegan nut milk ¾ cup walnuts
⅓ cup pistachios
6 dates, pitted
1 tablespoon flaxseed
1 teaspoon cinnamon
¼ teaspoon ginger powder 1 teaspoon vanilla extract Ice

Preparation

1. Combine all ingredients and blend until smooth. Slowly add milk as needed.

Nutrition facts per serving:

Calories 308, total fat 21 g, carbs 30 g,
Protein 7 g, sodium 92 mg

AYURVEDIC SMOOTHIE

Both ginger and turmeric are powerful anti-inflammatories believed to help prevent cancer and other serious conditions. This smoothie does not call for ice, because Ayurvedic medicine, the yogic science of health and nutrition, recommends avoiding cold foods.

Yields: 2 – Prep. Time: 5 min. – Cooking Time: 0 min.

Ingredients
1 banana
½ teaspoon turmeric
¼ teaspoon ginger
1 cup vegan milk
1 tablespoon maple syrup

Preparation
1. Combine all ingredients and blend until smooth. Slowly add milk as needed.

Nutrition facts per serving:
Calories 125, total fat 2 g, carbs 24 g,
Protein 4 g, sodium 62 mg

FIG SHAKE

With their sweet and unique flavor, figs are one of the treasures of the Mediterranean. They're also loaded with fiber and are a good source of magnesium, a mineral needed for restful sleep.

Yields: 2 – Prep. Time: 5 min. – Cooking Time: 0 min.

Ingredients 8 figs
2 bananas
1 cup vegan milk
1 teaspoon cinnamon
¼ teaspoon ginger, ground
Pinch cardamom
1 tablespoon maple syrup
¼ cup granola
Ice

Preparation

1. Combine all ingredients, except for the granola, and blend until smooth. Slowly add milk as needed.

2. Add granola and blend for a few seconds.

Nutrition facts per serving:
Calories 380, total fat 3 g, carbs 86 g, Protein 8 g, sodium 65 mg

WINTER BLUES

Seasonal Affective Disorder affects many of us. Luckily, there are ways to prevent the so-called winter blues. One of them is through diet. A diet high in omega-3 fatty acids, vitamin D, and probiotics can help you prevent winter depression, so add this smoothie to your routine come fall.

Yields: 2 – Prep. Time: 5 min. – Cooking Time: 0 min.

Ingredients
1 cup blueberries
1 packet acai puree
1 apple
1 cup vegan yogurt
1 tablespoon chia seeds
½ tablespoon flaxseeds
Ice

Preparation
1. Combine all ingredients and blend until smooth.

Nutrition facts per serving:
Calories 264, total fat 8 g, carbs 47 g,
Protein 5 g, sodium 27 mg

Green Smoothies

PINEAPPLE-MINT

This smoothie is just so refreshing, a perfect addition to a summer day. Fresh mint helps to soothe your stomach, while pineapple is great for your skin. Anti-inflammatory pineapple has even been shown to help with arthritis pain. Another friend for your stomach, celery helps to prevent bloating, so drink this delicious smoothie before a hot date.

Yields: 2 – Prep. Time: 5 min. – Cooking Time: 0 min.

Ingredients
1½ cup pineapple
½ cup fresh mint leaves 1 stalk celery, diced
½ cup coconut water
Ice

Preparation
1. Combine all ingredients and blend until smooth. Slowly add ice and coconut water as needed.

Nutrition facts per serving:
Calories 173, total fat 0 g, carbs 44 g,
Protein 1 g, sodium 36 mg

TUMMY TAMER

Probiotics from vegan yogurt combined with mint, ginger, and healthy fruits and veggies all work together to soothe your stomach. This smoothie can also work wonders for a bloated stomach.

Yields: 2 – Prep. Time: 5 min. – Cooking Time: 0 min.

Ingredients
1 cup vegan yogurt
½ cup coconut water 1 banana
½ cup pineapple 1 cup spinach
¼ cup mint leaves
½ lemon, juiced
1 tablespoon ginger, fresh
Ice

Preparation
1. Combine all ingredients and blend until smooth. Slowly add ice and coconut water as needed.

Nutrition facts per serving:
Calories 210, total fat 2 g, carbs 46 g,
Protein 5 g, sodium 42 mg

TROPICAL GREENS

This smoothie delivers the gorgeous flavors and colors of the tropics, plus all the nutrients. Pineapple and papaya do wonders for your digestion, while coconut water delivers some much-needed electrolytes.

Yields: 4 – Prep. Time: 5 min. – Cooking Time: 0 min.

Ingredients
½ cup pineapple
½ cup papaya, peeled and diced
1 mango
1 banana
2 dates, pitted
1 cup spinach
1 cup kale
1 cup coconut water

Preparation
1. Combine all ingredients and blend until smooth. Slowly add ice and coconut water as needed.

Nutrition facts per serving:
Calories 174, total fat 1 g, carbs 44 g,
Protein 1 g, sodium 108 mg

HERBAL REMEDY

Herbs are an overlooked green to add to smoothies! Not only are they packed with flavor, they're also full of vitamins and minerals. The herbs in this smoothie will especially help you to detox heavy metals from your system, while ginger serves as a diuretic, enhancing the detoxifying benefits.

Yields: 4 – Prep. Time: 5 min. – Cooking Time: 0 min.

Ingredients
1 green apple
1 cup pineapple
1 kiwi
2 dates, pitted
1 cup coconut water
1 cup spinach
½ cup cilantro
½ cup mint
1 tablespoon ginger
Ice

Preparation
1. Combine all ingredients and blend until smooth. Slowly add ice and coconut water as needed.

Nutrition facts per serving:
Calories 125, total fat <1 g, carbs 25 g,
Protein 1 g, sodium 24 mg

STRAWBERRY BASIL

Did you know that basil is antibacterial, antimicrobial, and antiinflammatory? It's also filled with antioxidants and may help to prevent depression—all the more reason to try this unique and delicious smoothie!

Yields: 2 – Prep. Time: 5 min. – Cooking Time: 0 min.

Ingredients
1 cup strawberries
½ cup basil leaves, fresh
½ cup vegan milk
2 dates, pitted
Ice

Preparation
1. Combine all ingredients and blend until smooth. Slowly add ice and milk as needed.

Nutrition facts per serving:
Calories 68, total fat 1 g, carbs 13 g,
Protein 3 g, sodium 31 mg

GINGER LIME

With citrus lime and antibiotic ginger, this smoothie will work wonders for your immune system.

Yields: 2 – Prep. Time: 5 min. – Cooking Time: 0 min.

Ingredients
1 green apple
1 kiwi
2 limes, juiced
1 cup spinach
1 tablespoon ginger, fresh
2 dates, pitted
Water
Ice

Preparation
1. Combine all ingredients and blend until smooth. Slowly add ice and water as needed.

Nutrition facts per serving:
Calories 118, total fat <1 g, carbs 30 g, Protein 2 g, sodium 16 mg

CREAMY GREENS

This smoothie is so creamy that it's practically ice cream. Avocado and banana deliver detoxifying fiber, while chia seeds add some protein and help you feel full. The perfect morning smoothie.

Yields: 2 – Prep. Time: 5 min. – Cooking Time: 0 min.

Ingredients 1 banana
1 avocado
1 cup pineapple
1 cup spinach
1 cup coconut water
2 dates
1 tablespoon chia seeds

Preparation
1. Combine all ingredients and blend until smooth. Slowly add ice and coconut water as needed.

Nutrition facts per serving:
Calories 347, total fat 13 g, carbs 60 g,
Protein 4 g, sodium 52 mg

GREEN TART

Some of us can't get enough of tart and tangy flavors. The tart green apples and vegan yogurt deliver all the flavor you need, while also working wonders for your digestive system. Meanwhile, limes and pomegranate seeds are here to support your immune system.

Yields: 2 – Prep. Time: 5 min. – Cooking Time: 0 min.

Ingredients

2 green apples
2 limes, juiced
1 cup vegan yogurt, plain
¼ cup pomegranate seeds
1 cup leafy greens
1 date, pitted
Ice

Preparation

1. Combine all ingredients and blend until smooth. Slowly add ice and coconut water as needed.

Nutrition facts per serving:

Calories 231, total fat 2 g, carbs 53 g,
Protein 5 g, sodium 28 mg

MORNING MATCHA

Matcha green tea isn't just one of the richest sources of antioxidants, it's also guaranteed to kick-start your morning. Avocado and coconut milk lend healthy fats that are great for your brain and skin and also help you feel full for hours. Drinking this smoothie in lieu of coffee will give you sustained energy all day.

Yields: 2 – Prep. Time: 5 min. – Cooking Time: 0 min.

Ingredients
2 teaspoons matcha powder
1 pear
1 cup pineapple
1 kiwi
½ avocado
½ cup spinach
1 cup coconut milk Ice (if needed) **Preparation**
1. Combine all ingredients and blend until smooth. Slowly add ice and coconut milk as needed.

Nutrition facts per serving:
Calories 376, total fat 20 g, carbs 50 g,
Protein 4 g, sodium 43 mg

Smoothie Bowls

57

SUNRISE SMOOTHIE BOWL

Smoothie bowls aren't just nutritious meals, they're works of art! This smoothie bowl combines tropical flavors and the beautiful color of the sunrise to help you start your morning.

Yields: 2 – Prep. Time: 5 min. – Cooking Time: 0 min.

Ingredients
½ cup papaya
½ cup pineapple
1 cup strawberries
1 banana, frozen
Coconut water (as needed) 1 tablespoon chia seeds
2 tablespoons coconut shreds

Preparation

1. Combine frozen banana with fruit and coconut water as needed. Blend until smooth.

2. Serve in a bowl topped with chia seeds, shredded coconut, and any other toppings you'd like.

Nutrition facts per serving:
Calories 348, total fat 6 g, carbs 76 g,
Protein 2 g, sodium 191 mg

CHOCOLATE MINT BOWL

This mint chocolate chip smoothie bowl is so delicious that it's practically dessert. The good news is that raw cocoa powder is high in antioxidants, while fresh mint is soothing for your stomach and helps to reduce bloating.

Yields: 2 – Prep. Time: 5 min. – Cooking Time: 0 min.

Ingredients
2 bananas, frozen
Handful mint leaves
2 tablespoons cocoa powder
Vegan nut milk (as needed)
½ cup carob chips

Preparation
1. Add bananas, mint, and cocoa powder to your blender. Blend on high, adding nut milk a little at a time until you have your desired consistency.

2. Mix in carob chips and serve immediately.

Nutrition facts per serving:
Calories 239, total fat 7 g, carbs 49 g,
Protein 1 g, sodium 15 mg

BANANA SPLIT BOWL

One of the best things about a vegan diet is that you can indulge all of your cravings without feeling guilty about it. Craving a banana split? No problem—try this delicious but healthy version.

Yields: 2 – Prep. Time: 5 min. – Cooking Time: 0 min.

Ingredients
2 bananas, frozen
1 banana
1 cup strawberries, plus extra for topping
Vegan whipped cream
Carob chips
Cherries
Almond milk (as needed)

Preparation
1. Add strawberries and frozen bananas to the blender. Blend together while slowly adding milk until you reach your desired consistency. It should be thick, but not too thick.

2. Serve topped with cherries, whipped cream, carob chips, banana, and anything else you might like.

Nutrition facts per serving:
Calories 314, total fat 14 g, carbs 51 g,
Protein 4 g, sodium 40 mg

NUTELLA BOWL

Who doesn't love chocolate and hazelnuts? Instead of eating Nutella by the jar, try eating this healthy smoothie bowl instead. Nutella may not be the healthiest thing in the world, but hazelnuts are actually loaded with vitamin E, B vitamins, and healthy fats. This bowl is guaranteed to satisfy and nourish.

Yields: 2 – Prep. Time: 5 min. – Cooking Time: 0 min.

Ingredients

2 bananas, frozen
¼ cup hazelnuts
2 tablespoons cocoa powder
Vegan nut milk (as needed)
1 tablespoon maple syrup (or to taste)

Preparation

1. Blend all ingredients together, adding nut milk a little at a time until you have your desired consistency.

Nutrition facts per serving:

Calories 315, total fat 20 g, carbs 35 g,
Protein 7 g, sodium 39 mg

IPANEMA BOWL

Acai bowls are one of the best things about Brazil. You can see Brazilians eating them by the beach and all over town. Not surprising, considering how delicious and nourishing these little purple berries are—super-high in antioxidants and a good source of omega fatty acids. You'll be feeling amazing after this smoothie bowl!

Yields: 2 – Prep. Time: 5 min. – Cooking Time: 0 min.

Ingredients
2 packs frozen acai pulp
2 bananas, frozen
1 mango
½ cup vegan milk
½ cup granola
Light agave nectar
Coconut shreds
3 strawberries, sliced

Preparation

1. Blend together the acai, mango, milk, and bananas until smooth.

2. Pour into a bowl and serve topped with agave nectar, strawberries, granola and shredded coconut.

Nutrition facts per serving:

Calories 446, total fat 13 g, carbs 81 g,
Protein 8 g, sodium 57 mg

BEAUTY BOWL

This yummy bowl is a filling meal that's also loaded with healthy fats and antioxidants to give you gorgeous, glowing skin.

Yields: 2 – Prep. Time: 5 min. – Cooking Time: 0 min.

Ingredients
2 bananas, frozen
1 pear
1 mango
1 cup spinach
2 tablespoons chia seeds
1 tablespoon nut butter
1 tablespoon flaxseed Goji berries
Pomegranate seeds
Orange juice (as needed)

Preparations

1. Combine flaxseed, nut butter, spinach and fruit in the blender. Blend until smooth, adding orange juice as needed.

2. Serve in bowls topped with chia seeds, pomegranate seeds, and goji berries.

Nutrition facts per serving:

Calories 374, total fat 11 g, carbs 73 g,
Protein 9 g, sodium 62 mg

OCEAN BREEZE

The health benefits of protein-packed spirulina cannot be overstated. Some have even called this algae the most nutrient-dense food on earth. Plus, this superfood gives this smoothie bowl a gorgeous color.

Yields: 2 – Prep. Time: 5 min. – Cooking Time: 0 min.

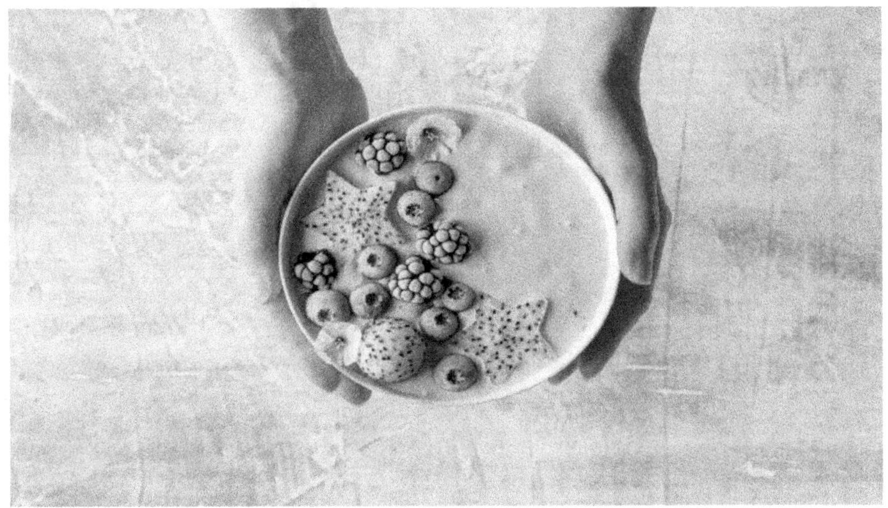

Ingredients
2 bananas, frozen
1 cup blueberries, plus more for topping
1 mango
Coconut water (as needed) 1 tablespoon chia seeds
1 teaspoon blue spirulina
Coconut shreds

Preparations
1. Combine fruit and spirulina in the blender. Blend until smooth, adding coconut water as needed.
2. Serve in bowls topped with chia seeds, coconut shreds, and more berries.

Nutrition facts per serving:
Calories 232, total fat 3 g, carbs 53 g, Protein 4 g, sodium 5 mg

STRAWBERRY OATMEAL

Loaded with protein and heart healthy fiber, oatmeal is the ideal breakfast. Add it to strawberries and banana in this super-simple smoothie bowl for a creamy, delicious meal.

Yields: 2 – Prep. Time: 5 min. – Cooking Time: 0 min.

Ingredients
2 bananas, frozen
1 cup strawberries, plus extra for topping
⅓ cup rolled oats
¼ teaspoon vanilla extract 1 tablespoon chia seeds
Almond milk (as needed)
Rose petals (optional)

Preparation
1. Combine fruit, oats, and vanilla in the blender. Blend until smooth, adding almond milk as needed.

2. Serve in bowls topped with chia seeds, more berries, and rose petals.

Nutrition facts per serving:
Calories 232, total fat 3 g, carbs 53 g,
Protein 4 g, sodium 5 mg

TURBO GREENS PROTEIN

Not everyone loves eating their greens, but they really *are* good for you!
If you're one of those who'd rather avoid them, try eating them disguised in
a delish smoothie! This smoothie is filled with vitamin C, antioxidants, and
enough greens to get you through the day.

Yields: 2 – Prep. Time: 5 min. – Cooking Time: 0 min.

Ingredients
2 bananas, frozen
1 cup mixed berries, plus extra for topping
1 kiwi, peeled
1 cup spinach
1 cup kale, stems removed
¼ cup quinoa, cooked 2 dates, pitted
1 tablespoon nut butter
1 tablespoon flaxseed
2 tablespoons chia seeds
Soy milk (as needed)

Preparation
1.   Combine fruit, nut butter, greens, and quinoa in the blender
and blend until smooth, adding soy milk as needed.
2.   Serve in bowls topped with chia seeds and berries.

Nutrition facts per serving:
Calories 317, total fat 8 g, carbs 60 g,
Protein 8 g, sodium 23 mg

DRAGON FRUIT BOWL

This exotic fruit is a work of art that's also filled with fiber, prebiotics, and vitamin C, so it's great for your digestive and immune systems. The beautiful bright pink color might even tempt some of the little ones into trying this bowl!

Yields: 2 – Prep. Time: 5 min. – Cooking Time: 0 min.

Ingredients
2 bananas, frozen
1 dragon fruit
1 star fruit, sliced
1 mango
2 tablespoons chia seeds
2 pineapple rings
Coconut shreds
Coconut water (as needed)

Preparation
1. In a blender, combine bananas, dragon fruit, and mango. Blend until smooth, adding coconut water as needed.

2. Serve in bowls topped with pineapple, chia seeds, star fruit, and coconut shreds.

Nutrition facts per serving:
Calories 356, total fat 13 g, carbs 66 g,
Protein 8 g, sodium 40 mg

KEY LIME PIE SMOOTHIE BOWL

Who says you can't have dessert for breakfast? This refreshing and indulgent breakfast smoothie bowl is a great way to supercharge your mornings.

Yields: 2 – Prep. Time: 5 min. – Cooking Time: 0 min.

Ingredients
3 tablespoons key lime juice
1 frozen banana ½ cup spinach
1 Granny Smith apple
1–2 tablespoons light agave nectar
Water

Preparation
1. Add the frozen banana to your blender and blend on low. Add water a tablespoon at a time, as needed, until the banana reaches a creamy consistency.

2. Add the remaining ingredients and blend again until creamy.

Nutrition facts per serving:
Calories 248, total fat <1 g, carbs 61 g,
Protein 2 g, sodium 0 mg

Dessert Smoothies

CINNAMON ROLL

Cinnamon rolls in the morning are sure to get everyone out of bed fast, but they're also loaded with sugar and simple carbs that give you an energy crash by noon. This smoothie has oats that help you maintain your energy all day long.

Yields: 2 – Prep. Time: 5 min. – Cooking Time: 0 min.

Ingredients

1 banana, frozen 1 cup vegan milk
½ cup rolled oats
1 tablespoon maple syrup
½ teaspoon cinnamon, ground, plus extra for topping
½ teaspoon vanilla extract
Vegan whipped cream

Preparation

1. Combine all ingredients and blend until smooth.
2. Serve topped with cinnamon and/or whipped cream.

Nutrition facts per serving:

Calories 375, total fat 17g, carbs 50 g,
Protein 9 g, sodium 78 mg

PEACHES AND CREAM

With this healthy, vitamin-C-packed smoothie, your skin will be as clear and creamy as peaches and cream.

Yields: 2 – Prep. Time: 5 min. – Cooking Time: 0 min.

Ingredients 2 peaches
1 cup vegan milk
⅓ cup rolled oats
1 tablespoon maple syrup
½ teaspoon vanilla extract
Pinch of cinnamon (optional)
Vegan whipped cream
Ice

Preparation

1. Combine all ingredients and blend until smooth.
2. Serve topped with cinnamon and whipped cream.

Nutrition facts per serving:
Calories 293, total fat 15 g, carbs 37 g,
Protein 5 g, sodium 76 mg

AUTUMN DELIGHT

This smoothie is filled with fiber and probiotics, so it's a great addition to a cleanse or just a good way to lower cholesterol. Not to mention it captures all the delicious flavors of fall!

Yields: 2 – Prep. Time: 5 min. – Cooking Time: 0 min.

Ingredients
2 apples, Honeycrisp is best 2 pears
1½ cups vegan yogurt, plain ¼ cup granola
2 tablespoons maple syrup
1 teaspoon cinnamon, ground
¼ teaspoon ginger, ground
Vegan whipped cream

Preparation
1. Combine all ingredients, except for the granola, and blend until smooth. Slowly add milk as needed.

2. When the smoothie is blended to your desired consistency, add granola and pulse for a few seconds. You just want to mix it in a little.

Nutrition facts per serving:
Calories 583, total fat 16 g, carbs 110 g,
Protein 10 g, sodium 29 mg

PIÑA COLADA

Piña colada is a tropical summer favorite. Serve this one around the pool and no one will have any idea it's filled with vitamin C and sugar free!

Yields: 2 – Prep. Time: 5 min. – Cooking Time: 0 min.

Ingredients
1 banana, frozen
1 cup pineapple
1 cup coconut yogurt, coconut flavor
1 tablespoon light agave nectar
Coconut shreds

Preparation
1. Combine all ingredients except for the coconut shreds and blend until smooth.
2. Serve topped with coconut shreds.

Nutrition facts per serving:
Calories 235, total fat <0 g, carbs 56 g,
Protein 5 g, sodium 41 mg

STRAWBERRY ROSEWATER

Rosewater is soothing for the central nervous system and also good for your skin. If you suffer from morning anxiety, this smoothie is a delicious way to start your day off right.

Yields: 2 – Prep. Time: 5 min. – Cooking Time: 0 min.

Ingredients
1 cup strawberries
1 cup vegan yogurt, plain
½ cup pomegranate seeds
1–2 tablespoons rosewater
2 dates, pitted
Ice

Preparation
1. Combine all ingredients and blend until smooth. Add ice as needed.

Nutrition facts per serving:
Calories 148, total fat 2 g, carbs 31 g,
Protein 4 g, sodium 15 mg

GINGERBREAD SMOOTHIE

Gingerbread is a delightful holiday treat, but those of us who are gluten intolerant don't get to indulge. This smoothie is the solution. Plus, the warming spices and vegan yogurt are great for your digestion.

Yields: 2 – Prep. Time: 5 min. – Cooking Time: 0 min.

Ingredients
1 banana
1 cup vegan yogurt, plain
2 tablespoons molasses
1 teaspoon cinnamon
¼ teaspoon ginger, ground
1 pinch allspice
Ice

Preparation
1. Combine all ingredients and blend until smooth. Add ice as needed.

Nutrition facts per serving:
Calories 196, total fat 2 g, carbs 42 g,
Protein 4 g, sodium 21 mg

PUMPKIN PIE JAR

Everyone loves sharing pumpkin pie around the holiday table, but did you know that pumpkin is actually loaded with vitamin A? That makes this smoothie a real treat for your skin as well as a delicious dessert.

Yields: 2 – Prep. Time: 5 min. – Cooking Time: 0 min.

Ingredients
1 banana, frozen
½ cup pumpkin puree
1 cup vegan milk, vanilla
1 tablespoon molasses
1 teaspoon pumpkin pie spices
Vegan whipped cream

Preparation
1. Combine all ingredients and blend until smooth.

Nutrition facts per serving:
Calories 282, total fat 14 g, carbs 37 g,
Protein 6 g, sodium 67 mg

HOT CHOCOLATE

Not all smoothies have to be cold! This warm smoothie is a healthier take on hot chocolate. Warm oats are guaranteed to give you sustained energy for hours.

Yields: 2 – Prep. Time: 8 hours – Cooking Time: 5 min.

Ingredients
1 cup vegan milk
½ cup rolled oats
2 tablespoons cocoa powder
1 tablespoon molasses

Preparation

1. Mix all ingredients together and allow to soak overnight in the fridge.

2. In the morning, add the ingredients to the blender and blend until smooth.

3. Heat in a saucepan and serve warm.

Nutrition facts per serving:
Calories 244, total fat 5 g, carbs 36 g,
Protein 10 g, sodium 60 mg

CHOCOLATE CHERRY

Come Valentine's Day, you may find yourself craving chocolate covered cherries. Why don't you try this vegan, sugar-free smoothie instead? Between cherries and cocoa powder, this smoothie is loaded with antioxidants, while healthy fats come courtesy of avocado.

Yields: 2 – Prep. Time: 5 min. – Cooking Time: 0 min.

Ingredients
1 cup sweet cherries, pitted
1 cup vegan milk
2 tablespoons raw cocoa½ avocado
1 tablespoon maple syrup
Carob chips (optional topping)
Ice

Preparation

1. Combine all ingredients and blend until smooth.

Nutrition facts per serving:

Calories 265, total fat 8 g, carbs 46 g,
Protein 7 g, sodium 66 mg

CARROT CAKE

Parents have long been using carrot cake to trick kids into eating their veggies. This smoothie is a super-easy vegan way to do the same. Carrots are loaded with vitamin A and fiber, while vegan yogurt and spices work wonders for your gut microbiome and overall digestive health.

Yields: 2 – Prep. Time: 5 min. – Cooking Time: 0 min.

Ingredients
1 banana
1 cup shredded carrots
1 cup vegan yogurt
2 tablespoons molasses
½ teaspoon cinnamon, ground
⅛ teaspoon ginger, ground
1 dash nutmeg
Water (as needed)
Ice (as needed)

Preparation
1. Combine all ingredients and blend until smooth.

Nutrition facts per serving:
Calories 240, total fat 2 g, carbs 52 g, Protein 5 g, sodium 108 mg

Cooking Conversion Charts

1. Measuring Equivalent Chart

Type	Imperial	Imperial	Metric
Weight	1 dry ounce		28g
	1 pound	16 dry ounces	0.45 kg
Volume	1 teaspoon		5 ml
	1 dessert spoon	2 teaspoons	10 ml
	1 tablespoon	3 teaspoons	15 ml
	1 Australian tablespoon	4 teaspoons	20 ml
	1 fluid ounce	2 tablespoons	30 ml
	1 cup	16 tablespoons	240 ml
	1 cup	8 fluid ounces	240 ml
	1 pint	2 cups	470 ml
	1 quart	2 pints	0.95 l
	1 gallon	4 quarts	3.8 l
Length	1 inch		2.54 cm

* Numbers are rounded to the closest equivalent

2. Oven Temperature Equivalent Chart

Fahrenheit (°F)	Celsius (°C)	Gas Mark
220	100	
225	110	1/4
250	120	1/2
275	140	1
300	150	2
325	160	3
350	180	4
375	190	5
400	200	6
425	220	7
450	230	8
475	250	9
500	260	

* Celsius (°C) = T (°F)-32] * 5/9
** Fahrenheit (°F) = T (°C) * 9/5 + 32
*** Numbers are rounded to the closest equivalent

ABOUT THE AUTHOR

Insert author bio text here. Insert author bio text here